Why Your Brain Won't Let You Feel Safe

by Rowan Blake

The Hidden Science Behind Modern Anxiety

Copyright ©2025 by RowanBlake.

This publication is intended for informational and educational purposes only. It is not a substitute for professional therapy, mental health treatment, or medical advice. If you are experiencing psychological distress, trauma, or symptoms of a mental health condition, please consult a licensed mental health professional.

Every effort has been made to ensure the accuracy of the information contained in this book as of the publication date. However, psychological understanding evolves, and the author assumes no responsibility for errors or omissions or for the outcomes resulting from the use of this material.

Table Of Contents

Introduction

You're tired of feeling like you're waiting for the other shoe to drop. Tired of scanning every room you walk into, looking for exits and threats that probably aren't there. Tired of your heart racing when someone raises their voice, even when they're not angry at you. Tired of feeling like you're too much and not enough at the same time.

You've tried everything. You've read the self-help books that tell you to "just think positive." You've done the meditation apps that promise inner peace in ten minutes a day. You've tried therapy, maybe more than once. Some things helped a little, for a while. But that feeling in your chest - that tight, watchful, never-quite-relaxed feeling - it's still there.

Maybe you've been told you're "too sensitive" or that you "worry too much." Maybe you've been told to "get over it" or "let it go." Maybe you've started to believe that this is just who you are - the anxious one, the one who can't handle stress, the one who makes mountains out of molehills.

But what if none of that is true?

What if that feeling in your chest isn't a character flaw or a sign of weakness? What if it's actually your nervous system doing exactly what it was designed to do - protect you from danger? What if your brain learned, somewhere along the way, that the world isn't safe, and now it's working overtime to keep you alive?

What if you're not broken? What if you're having a completely normal response to things that shouldn't have happened to you?

Here's what I know after years of working with people who feel exactly like you do: Your nervous system is not the enemy. It's been your protector, your guardian, your early warning system. It's been scanning for danger and preparing you to fight, flee, or freeze because at some point in your life, you needed those responses to survive.

The problem is, your nervous system doesn't know the difference between then and now. It doesn't know that you're safe now, even when you are. It's still operating from old information, old fears, old threats that may no longer exist.

You might be wondering what happened to make your system so vigilant. Maybe you remember exactly what it was - the divorce when you were eight, the car accident when you were sixteen, the relationship that left you questioning everything you thought you knew about love.

Maybe it wasn't one big thing but a thousand smaller ones - growing up in a house where you never knew what mood someone would be in, having a parent who loved you but couldn't show it in ways you could understand, being the kid who got picked on at school while the adults looked the other way.

Or maybe you can't put your finger on it at all. Maybe your childhood looked fine from the outside, your family seemed normal, and you have no idea why you feel this way. That's okay too. Sometimes our nervous systems pick up on things our conscious minds don't remember or didn't recognize as threatening at the time.

What matters isn't figuring out exactly what happened. What matters is understanding that your nervous system learned to be afraid, and now you can teach it to feel safe again.

This isn't about positive thinking or pushing through the fear. This isn't about being stronger or tougher or more resilient. This is about understanding how your body and brain work together, how trauma gets stored in your nervous system, and how you can work with your body's own healing wisdom to find the peace you've been searching for.

You don't need to be fixed because you're not broken. You need to be understood, and you need tools that actually work with how your nervous system functions, not against it.

Maybe right now you're thinking, "This sounds too good to be true. I've tried everything, and nothing works." I get it. When you've been living with anxiety, hypervigilance, or that constant feeling of impending doom for years, it's hard to believe that things can really change.

But they can. Not overnight, and not without effort, but they absolutely can.

Your nervous system is incredibly intelligent, but it's also incredibly adaptable. The same system that learned to be afraid can learn to be calm. The same system that learned to expect danger can learn to recognize safety. It just needs the right information and the right approach.

In these pages, you'll discover why your brain keeps you stuck in survival mode and how to gently guide it back to a place of calm. You'll learn why some healing approaches work and others don't. You'll understand why willpower isn't enough and what actually is.

Most importantly, you'll learn that healing is possible. Not just managing your symptoms or coping better, but actually healing - living with a nervous system that trusts you're safe, relationships that nourish you, and a life that feels like your own.

You picked up this book for a reason. Maybe something in you is ready to try a different way. Maybe you're tired of just surviving and ready to start thriving. Maybe you're ready to discover that the very sensitivity and awareness that sometimes feels like a curse can actually become your greatest strength.

Your nervous system has been protecting you for so long. Now it's time to learn how to help it relax, how to show it that you're safe now, and how to build a life where that safety isn't just a hope but a lived reality.

The journey starts with understanding. And understanding starts right here, right now, with the recognition that you're not too much, you're not not enough, and you're definitely not broken.

You're ready to heal. Your nervous system is ready to learn. And the life you've been dreaming of - the one where you feel peaceful, confident, and authentically yourself - is waiting for you.

Let's begin.

Chapter 1: The Safety Paradox - Why Your Stone Age Brain Lives in a Digital World

You check your phone at 2 AM. Your heart races. You scan your bedroom for threats that don't exist. Welcome to the evolutionary mismatch that's hijacking your peace.

If this sounds familiar, you're not alone. Every day, millions of people wake up feeling like they're in danger when they're perfectly safe. They check their doors three times before bed. Their stomachs twist when they see an email from their boss. They feel their chest tighten when walking into a crowded room. And the strangest part? They can't figure out why.

Here's what nobody tells you: your brain is doing exactly what it was designed to do. The problem isn't that something is wrong with you. The problem is that your brain is a masterpiece of survival engineering that hasn't gotten the memo that the world has changed.

Let me explain what's really happening inside your head.

Your brain has been keeping humans alive for millions of years. Back when your ancestors lived in caves and hunted woolly mammoths, survival was simple. See a tiger? Run. Hear a strange noise at night? Wake up and grab your spear. Meet a stranger from another tribe? Be ready to fight or flee. Your brain got really, really good at this job.

The part of your brain that kept your ancestors alive is called the amygdala. Think of it as your personal body-guard. This bodyguard never sleeps, never takes a vacation, and never assumes everything is fine. Its only job is to scan for danger and sound the alarm when it finds something that might hurt you.

Your amygdala is about the size of an almond, but it packs more punch than any other part of your brain. When it spots danger, it can flood your entire body with stress hor-mones faster than you can blink. It can make your heart pound, your breathing shallow, and your muscles tense, all without asking your permission.

This system worked perfectly when danger looked like sharp teeth and claws. But here's the thing: your amygdala hasn't evolved much since then. It still thinks you're living in caves, dodging predators and competing for scarce re-sources.

Meanwhile, you're living in a world of smartphones, social media, 24-hour news cycles, and endless demands on your time and attention. Your ancient brain is trying to navigate a modern world with stone-age software.

Let me paint you a picture of what this looks like in real life.

You're lying in bed, finally ready to sleep after a long day. Your phone buzzes with a text message. Before you even read it, your amygdala springs into action. "Alert! Something is happening!" it screams. Your heart rate jumps. Your breathing gets shallow. Stress hormones start pumping through your bloodstream.

The text is from your friend asking if you want to grab coffee tomorrow. Completely harmless. But your amygdala doesn't know that. It just knows that something unexpected happened, and in cave-person times, unexpected things were often dangerous.

Or picture this: you're at work, and you see an email from your boss with the subject line "We need to talk." Your amygdala doesn't wait to read the email. It immediately assumes the worst. "Danger! Threat to your survival!" it shouts. Your stomach drops. Your palms get sweaty. Your mind starts racing through all the terrible possibilities.

The email turns out to be about a new project your boss wants your input on. Again, completely harmless. But your brain treated it like a life-or-death situation.

This is what I call the "caveman brain in corporate clothes" problem. Your threat detection system is like having a smoke alarm that goes off when you burn toast. It's trying to protect you, but it's way too sensitive for your actual environment.

Let's talk about how this threat detection system actually works, because understanding it is the first step to taming it.

When your amygdala spots something it thinks might be dangerous, it sends an emergency signal to another part of your brain called the hypothalamus. The hypothalamus is like your brain's 911 dispatcher. It immediately calls in the troops.

First, it activates your sympathetic nervous system. This is your body's gas pedal. It tells your adrenal glands to dump stress hormones into your bloodstream. The main players are cortisol, adrenaline, and norepinephrine.

Cortisol is like your body's built-in alarm system. It raises your blood sugar, increases your blood pressure, and sharpens your focus. Adrenaline is pure rocket fuel. It makes your heart race and gives you a burst of energy. Norepinephrine acts like a spotlight, making you hyper-aware of everything around you.

All of this happens in milliseconds, long before your thinking brain has a chance to figure out what's actually going on.

In cave-person times, this system was lifesaving. If a predator appeared, you needed to run faster, hit harder, and think quicker than ever before. These stress hormones gave you superpowers.

But here's the problem: your brain can't tell the difference between a real tiger and a metaphorical one. A nasty comment on social media triggers the same biological response as facing down a wild animal. An argument with your partner floods your system with the same chemicals that helped your ancestors survive actual physical attacks.

Your modern world is full of these fake tigers. Every notification on your phone is a potential threat. Every deadline at work is a survival challenge. Every social situation is a test of whether you'll be accepted by the tribe or cast out to die alone.

Your brain treats a job interview the same way it would treat being stalked by a predator. It responds to financial stress like you're facing starvation. It reacts to relationship problems as if your very survival depends on fixing them immediately.

And because these modern threats never really go away, your threat detection system never gets to rest. You're not just dealing with one tiger that you can either fight off or escape from. You're dealing with an endless parade of potential dangers that your brain interprets as life-threatening.

This is why you might find yourself lying awake at 3 AM, your mind racing through worst-case scenarios about tomorrow's presentation. Your amygdala has decided that this presentation is a matter of life and death, and it's keeping you alert and ready for battle.

This is why you might feel your chest tighten when you walk into a room full of strangers. Your brain is scanning for signs that these people might reject you, which in ancient times could have meant being kicked out of your tribe and left to survive alone.

This is why you might check your email obsessively, even when you're supposed to be relaxing. Your brain has learned that missing important information could be dangerous, so it keeps you on high alert for any new developments.

Your brain isn't malfunctioning. It's doing exactly what millions of years of evolution programmed it to do. The problem is that the world changed faster than your brain could adapt.

But here's the good news: understanding this is the first step to reclaiming your peace of mind. When you realize that your anxiety isn't a character flaw or a sign of weakness, but rather an ancient survival system working overtime, everything changes.

You're not broken. You're not crazy. You're not weak. You're a modern human with an ancient brain, trying to navigate a world that your threat detection system doesn't understand.

The racing heart when you check your phone? That's your amygdala trying to protect you from danger that isn't there. The knot in your stomach when you think about tomorrow's challenges? That's stress hormones preparing you for battles you don't need to fight. The restless energy that keeps you from relaxing? That's your sympathetic nervous system keeping you ready for threats that exist only in your imagination.

Once you understand this, you can start to work with your brain instead of against it. You can learn to recognize when your ancient survival system is overreacting to modern situations. You can develop skills to calm your threat detection system and teach it the difference between real danger and false alarms.

Your anxiety isn't your enemy. It's a loyal bodyguard that's been working the night shift for millions of years. It just needs some updated training for the modern world.

In the next chapter, we'll explore what happens when this threat detection system has been running on high alert for too long, and how chronic hypervigilance actually changes the structure of your brain. But for now, just knowing that your feelings of unease aren't your fault is enough.

Your brain won't let you feel safe because it's trying to keep you alive. That's not a bug in the system. That's a feature that's been protecting humans since the beginning of time. The key is learning how to update the software so it works better in your current reality.

Chapter 2 : The Invisible Prison - How Chronic Hyper-vigilance Rewires Your Brain

Your brain has been playing a horror movie soundtrack for months, maybe years. Here's how to change the channel.

Imagine your brain is like a muscle. If you spend months lifting heavy weights, your muscles get bigger and stronger. But what if the weight you've been lifting is anxiety? What if your brain has been practicing fear for so long that being scared has become its default setting?

This is exactly what happens when your threat detection system stays switched on for too long. Your brain literally changes shape. The parts that handle fear get bigger and stronger, while the parts that help you think clearly and stay calm get smaller and weaker.

Scientists call this neuroplasticity, which is just a fancy way of saying your brain can rewire itself based on how you use it. This is usually great news. It means you can learn new skills, form new habits, and recover from injuries. But when your brain practices anxiety day after day, neuroplasticity works against you.

Let me explain what's happening inside your head when hyper-vigilance takes over.

Remember the amygdala from the last chapter? That almond-sized alarm system that's supposed to keep you safe? When you live in a constant state of alert, your amygdala starts growing. It's like a security guard who keeps getting promoted because there's always some new threat to worry about.

The bigger your amygdala gets, the more sensitive it becomes. It starts seeing danger everywhere. A car backfiring sounds like a gunshot. A friend's delayed text response means they're angry at you. A headache becomes a sign of a serious medical condition.

At the same time, another part of your brain starts shrinking. This part is called the prefrontal cortex, and it's your brain's CEO. It handles logical thinking, decision-making, and emotional regulation. It's the part that's supposed to tell your amygdala, "Hey, calm down, that's just a car backfiring."

But when the prefrontal cortex gets smaller, it can't do its job as well. Your brain's alarm system gets louder while your brain's voice of reason gets quieter. It's like having a smoke alarm that goes off every time you cook dinner, but the battery in your common sense detector is always dead.

This creates what I call the hypervigilance trap. The more anxious you feel, the more your brain rewires itself to feel anxious. It's a vicious cycle that can feel impossible to break.

Sarah is a perfect example of how this works. She's a successful marketing executive who should feel proud of her achievements. Instead, she hasn't taken a real vacation in three years. Even when she's at a beach resort, her mind is racing. She checks her work email every few minutes. She lies awake at night thinking about projects that are going fine. She can't enjoy a beautiful sunset because she's mentally rehearsing tomorrow's presentation.

Sarah's brain has been practicing anxiety for so long that relaxation feels dangerous. Her amygdala has learned that letting her guard down might mean missing something important. So even when she's in paradise, her brain keeps playing that horror movie soundtrack.

Then there's Maria, a mother of two young children. She loves her kids more than anything in the world, but she can't stop checking on them while they sleep. She tiptoes into their rooms multiple times each night, putting her hand near their faces to make sure they're breathing. During the day, she constantly imagines worst-case scenarios. What if they get hurt at school? What if they're not developing normally? What if she's not a good enough mother?

Maria's hypervigilance feels like love, but it's actually her threat detection system gone haywire. Her brain has decided that being a good mother means being constantly worried about every possible danger.

And there's Jennifer, a perfectionist who spends hours crafting emails that should take five minutes to write. She reads every message ten times before hitting send, looking for typos or phrases that might be misunderstood. She stays late at work not because she has too much to do, but because she can't stop double-checking her work. She's terrified of making a mistake that might make people think less of her.

Jennifer's brain has learned that perfection equals safety. Making a mistake feels like a threat to her survival, so her amygdala keeps her on high alert, scanning for every possible error.

What Sarah, Maria, and Jennifer don't realize is that their brains have been rewiring themselves to be anxious. Every time they give in to the urge to check their email, peek at their sleeping children, or rewrite that email for the tenth time, they're teaching their brains that these behaviors are necessary for survival.

This is what scientists call the sensitization effect. Each false alarm makes your brain more sensitive to the next potential threat. It's like having a car alarm that gets more sensitive every time it goes off. Eventually, a gentle breeze is enough to set it off.

Your brain also develops something called a default mode network. This is what your mind does when you're not actively focused on something specific. In a healthy brain, the default mode is usually peaceful. You might daydream, reflect on pleasant memories, or just exist in the present moment.

But when hypervigilance takes over, your default mode becomes worry mode. Instead of resting when you have downtime, your brain immediately starts scanning for problems. You can't take a shower without your mind racing through your to-do list. You can't watch a movie without thinking about tomorrow's challenges. Even during meditation, your thoughts keep jumping to potential threats.

This constant mental activity is exhausting. Your brain is like a computer with too many programs running in the background. It starts to slow down and overheat. This is why people with chronic anxiety often feel tired even when they haven't done anything physically demanding.

The hormonal effects make everything worse. When your threat detection system is constantly activated, your body keeps pumping out stress hormones like cortisol. In small doses, cortisol is helpful. It gives you energy and focus when you need it. But when cortisol levels stay high for months or years, it starts damaging your body and brain.

High cortisol interferes with sleep, which means your brain can't properly process and store memories from the day. This is why anxious people often have trouble remembering things or feel like their thoughts are foggy. Your brain needs sleep to file away important information and delete the mental clutter, but anxiety keeps interrupting this process.

Cortisol also suppresses your immune system, which is why people under chronic stress get sick more often. It interferes with digestion, causing stomach problems. It affects your ability to regulate emotions, making you more likely to snap at people you care about or cry over small disappointments.

For women, these effects are even more complicated because of monthly hormone cycles. Estrogen and progesterone levels naturally rise and fall throughout the month, and these changes interact with your stress response system in ways that can amplify anxiety.

During the week before your period, progesterone levels drop rapidly. Progesterone has a calming effect on the brain, so when it suddenly disappears, your amygdala becomes even more sensitive than usual. This is why many women notice their anxiety gets worse right before their period, even if everything else in their life is going fine.

Pregnancy and the postpartum period create their own unique challenges. During pregnancy, your body produces massive amounts of hormones to support your growing baby. These hormones can make your threat detection system hyperactive, which might seem like a problem but actually serves an important purpose. A pregnant woman needs to be extra careful about potential dangers to protect her unborn child.

The problem comes after the baby is born. Your hormone levels crash dramatically, leaving your nervous system destabilized. At the same time, you're dealing with sleep deprivation, major life changes, and the enormous responsibility of keeping a tiny human alive. It's no wonder that new mothers often feel overwhelmed and anxious.

Women also tend to have a different stress response than men. While men typically show more fight-or-flight responses, women are more likely to "tend and befriend." This means that when women feel threatened, they often try to fix problems by taking care of others or seeking social support.

This sounds healthier than fighting or running away, but it can create its own problems. Women who tend and befriend under stress often become people-pleasers. They take on extra responsibilities to help others feel better, even when they're already overwhelmed. They have trouble setting boundaries because saying no feels selfish or dangerous.

People-pleasing might seem like kindness, but it's actually a survival strategy. Your brain learns that keeping others happy reduces the chance that they'll reject you or become a threat. So you say yes when you want to say no, you smile when you're feeling frustrated, and you put everyone else's needs before your own.

This creates a chronic low-level threat state. You're constantly monitoring other people's moods and adjusting your behavior to keep them happy. Your amygdala stays partially activated all the time, scanning for signs that someone might be upset with you.

The perfectionism we see in people like Jennifer works the same way. Perfectionism feels like a high standard, but it's actually a fear response. Your brain decides that making mistakes is dangerous, so it keeps you hypervigilant about every detail. You check and recheck your work not because you care about quality, but because your amygdala has labeled errors as threats to your survival.

Here's what makes this whole situation particularly cruel: the harder you try to control your anxiety, the stronger it often gets. When you check your email for the fifteenth time, you're teaching your brain that checking email is necessary for safety. When you rewrite that email for the tenth time, you're reinforcing the idea that imperfection is dangerous.

Your brain doesn't understand that you're trying to reduce anxiety. It just sees that every time you feel anxious, you take some protective action, and then you feel temporarily better. So it concludes that the anxiety was justified and the protective action was necessary.

This is why willpower alone isn't enough to overcome chronic hypervigilance. Your brain has been practicing anxiety for so long that it's become automatic. Telling yourself to "just relax" is like telling your heart to stop beating. Your nervous system has learned these patterns at a level deeper than conscious thought.

But here's the hope: if your brain can learn to be anxious, it can also learn to be calm. The same neuroplasticity that created your hypervigilance can be used to reverse it. The parts of your brain that have grown sensitive to threat can be retrained to recognize safety. The prefrontal cortex that has been overwhelmed can be strengthened to regain control.

This isn't about positive thinking or pretending everything is fine. It's about understanding that your brain is incredibly adaptable, and the patterns that feel so fixed and permanent right now can actually be changed with the right approach.

Your brain has been training itself to be anxious, but you can retrain it for calm. The horror movie soundtrack doesn't have to play forever. With patience and the right tools, you can teach your brain to change the channel.

Chapter 3 : The Childhood Safety Blueprint - How Your Past Programs Your Present

At age 4, you learned whether the world was safe or dangerous. Your nervous system still remembers that lesson.

You might not remember learning this lesson. You probably can't point to a specific moment when your brain decided whether people could be trusted or whether you were worthy of love and protection. But somewhere in those early years, your developing nervous system was taking notes about how the world works.

Every interaction with your caregivers was like a data point in a massive research project. When you cried, did someone come to comfort you? When you were scared, did someone help you feel safe? When you made mistakes, were you met with patience or anger? When you needed attention, did you get it consistently or only sometimes?

Your little brain was constantly asking: "Am I safe here? Can I count on these people? What do I need to do to survive in this family?"

The answers to these questions became the blueprint for how your nervous system would respond to the world for the rest of your life.

This isn't anyone's fault. Your parents were probably doing the best they could with what they knew and what they had experienced in their own childhoods. But understanding how these early patterns formed is crucial to understanding why your brain might not let you feel safe now, even when you're surrounded by people who love you and living a life that should feel secure.

Let's start with how a baby's nervous system learns to regulate itself.

When you were born, your brain was incredibly underdeveloped compared to other animals. A baby deer can walk within hours of being born. A baby bird knows how to chirp for food. But human babies are completely helpless for years. This isn't an accident. It's because humans have the most complex brains on the planet, and that complexity takes time to develop.

For the first several years of life, you couldn't regulate your own emotions. When you were hungry, scared, or uncomfortable, you had no choice but to cry and hope that someone would help you. Your nervous system was like a car without a steering wheel, completely dependent on your caregivers to navigate the world.

Your caregivers weren't just taking care of your physical needs. They were actually helping to build the emotional regulation system in your brain. Every time they responded to your distress with comfort and care, they were teaching your nervous system that upset feelings don't last forever, that help is available, and that you're worth caring for.

This process is called co-regulation, and it's one of the most important things that happens in early childhood. Your caregivers were like emotional training wheels, helping you learn how to manage big feelings until your own brain developed enough to do it independently.

But what if your caregivers were overwhelmed, distracted, or dealing with their own trauma? What if they were loving but inconsistent? What if they were doing their best but didn't understand what you needed?

When caregivers can't provide consistent co-regulation, children develop what psychologists call insecure attachment patterns. These aren't character flaws or permanent damage. They're survival strategies that your young brain developed to cope with an unpredictable or overwhelming environment.

Let me explain the different patterns that children develop and how they might show up in your adult life.

Some children learn that they can't count on their caregivers to be emotionally available. Maybe their parents were loving but overwhelmed with work stress, financial problems, or their own mental health challenges. Maybe they were physically present but emotionally distant. These children often develop what's called anxious attachment.

As an adult with anxious attachment, you might find yourself constantly worried about whether people really care about you. You might text someone multiple times if they don't respond right away, convinced that they're angry or losing interest. You might have trouble trusting that relationships are stable, always looking for signs that people are about to leave you.

Your nervous system learned early that love and attention aren't guaranteed, so it stays hypervigilant for signs of rejection or abandonment. Even in healthy relationships, your amygdala might sound the alarm anytime your partner seems distant or distracted.

Other children learn that expressing their needs or emotions upsets their caregivers. Maybe their parents were dealing with their own trauma and couldn't handle a child's big emotions. Maybe they were taught that showing feelings was weak or inappropriate. These children often develop avoidant attachment.

As an adult with avoidant attachment, you might have trouble getting close to people or asking for help when you need it. You might pride yourself on being independent and self-sufficient, but secretly feel lonely or disconnected. You might shut down emotionally during conflicts or have difficulty expressing your feelings even to people you love.

Your nervous system learned that emotional needs are dangerous or burdensome, so it tries to minimize them. But the need for connection doesn't go away just because you learned to suppress it.

Some children experience caregiving that's both loving and frightening, often because their caregivers are dealing with their own unresolved trauma. These parents might be warm and nurturing one moment, then explosive or unpredictable the next. Children in these situations often develop disorganized attachment.

As an adult with disorganized attachment, relationships might feel simultaneously essential and terrifying. You might desperately want closeness but panic when you actually get it. You might find yourself drawn to people who are emotionally unavailable or even harmful, because un-predictability feels familiar even though it's painful.

Your nervous system learned that the people who are supposed to protect you can also be sources of threat, creating a constant internal conflict between the need for connection and the fear of being hurt.

The lucky children are those who experience secure attachment. Their caregivers are consistently responsive, emotionally available, and able to help them through difficult emotions. These children learn that they're worthy of love, that their feelings matter, and that relationships can be trusted.

But even people with generally secure attachment can have their nervous systems shaped by specific experiences or family patterns. Maybe your parents were loving but anxious, and you absorbed their worry about the world. Maybe they were caring but perfectionistic, and you learned that love was conditional on being "good."

Here's something crucial to understand: these patterns were created by experiences you can't consciously remember. Most of our attachment patterns are formed before age 3, long before we have the language or cognitive ability to make sense of what's happening to us.

This is the difference between implicit and explicit memory. Explicit memories are the ones you can consciously recall, like your first day of school or a family vacation. Implicit memories are stored in your body and nervous system without any narrative or timeline attached to them.

You might feel unsafe in certain situations without having any idea why. You might have a strong physical reaction to someone's tone of voice that reminds you unconsciously of something from your past. You might find yourself repeating relationship patterns that don't make logical sense but feel familiar at a deep level.

This is why you can't think your way out of these patterns. They're not stored in the logical, verbal part of your brain. They're embedded in the survival-oriented parts that developed first and fastest.

For many people, especially women, these early patterns get reinforced by cultural messages about safety and worth. Girls are often taught from a very young age to prioritize other people's comfort over their own needs. They learn to be "good girls" who are quiet, compliant, and focused on making others happy.

This might seem like positive social conditioning, but it can create chronic anxiety. When a girl learns that her worth depends on being perfect and making others comfortable, her nervous system starts treating any sign of disapproval as a threat to survival.

Many women grow up with an inner critic that sounds remarkably like early voices of authority. Maybe you hear your mother's anxious warnings about all the things that could go wrong. Maybe you hear your father's frustration when you didn't meet his expectations. Maybe you hear a teacher's impatience when you asked too many questions.

This inner critic feels like it's protecting you by pointing out all your flaws and mistakes before anyone else can. But it's actually keeping your threat detection system constantly activated. You're living with a critical voice in your head that never takes a break from finding problems.

The messages girls receive about physical safety can be particularly damaging to their overall sense of security. From a young age, girls are often warned about strangers, taught to be careful about how they dress, and given the message that the world is full of people who might hurt them.

These safety messages are often well-intentioned, but they can create a chronic sense of vulnerability. When you grow up believing that you're constantly at risk and that your safety depends on being hypervigilant and controlling your behavior perfectly, it's no wonder that your nervous system might struggle to ever truly relax.

Mother-daughter relationships often carry forward patterns of anxiety across generations. Mothers who struggled with their own safety and worth often unconsciously pass these concerns on to their daughters. They might be overprotective because they know how dangerous the world can be for women. They might be critical because they want their daughters to be prepared for a world that will judge them harshly.

But children don't understand the difference between protection and anxiety, between preparation and fear. They just absorb the emotional tone of their environment and assume that's how the world works.

This is where epigenetics comes in. Scientists have discovered that trauma and chronic stress can actually change which genes get activated and passed down to the next generation. Your grandparents' experiences of war, poverty, or persecution might have created changes in their stress response system that were passed down to your parents and then to you.

This doesn't mean you're doomed to repeat your family's patterns. It just means that your nervous system might be more sensitive or reactive than someone whose family history was less traumatic. You might need more support and different strategies to help your brain learn that you're safe now.

It's important to understand that not all of these patterns come from dramatic trauma. Sometimes the most damaging experiences are the quiet ones that nobody talks about. Emotional neglect can be just as harmful as abuse, but it's much harder to identify because it's about what didn't happen rather than what did.

Maybe your parents were physically present but emotionally unavailable because they were dealing with depression, addiction, or their own trauma. Maybe they loved you but didn't know how to show it in ways you could understand. Maybe they were caring but overwhelmed by the demands of work and survival.

Children in these situations often develop a sense that they're too much or not enough. They might become hypervigilant about other people's moods, constantly trying to figure out how to get the love and attention they need.

They might learn to suppress their own needs and feelings because expressing them feels dangerous or futile.

The key thing to remember is that none of this was your fault. You were a child doing your best to survive and get your needs met in whatever environment you found yourself in. The strategies you developed made perfect sense given what you were dealing with.

But those same strategies might not be serving you now. The hypervigilance that helped you navigate an unpredictable childhood might be making it hard for you to relax in your current relationships. The people-pleasing that kept you safe in your family might be exhausting you in your adult life.

Understanding where these patterns came from is the first step in changing them. When you realize that your anxiety about relationships isn't really about your current partner, but about old fears of abandonment, you can start to respond differently. When you recognize that your inner critic is using your mother's worried voice, you can begin to separate her fears from your actual reality.

Your nervous system learned its safety rules very early, in an environment where you had no choice but to adapt to whatever was available. But you're not that powerless child anymore. You have choices now that you didn't have then.

You can teach your nervous system new rules about safety, love, and worth. You can provide yourself with the consistent care and attention that maybe you didn't get enough of as a child. You can learn to be the calm, reliable presence for your own nervous system that your caregivers might not have been able to be.

This process is sometimes called reparenting, and it's one of the most powerful ways to heal these early patterns. Instead of waiting for someone else to make you feel safe and loved, you can learn to provide those feelings for yourself.

Your past programmed your present, but it doesn't have to determine your future.

Chapter 4 : The Hidden Body Conversation - What Your Physical Symptoms Are Really Telling You

Your headaches aren't about your head. Your stomach issues aren't about your stomach. They're your body's way of saying "I don't feel safe."

If you've been to doctor after doctor trying to figure out why you're always tired, why your stomach hurts for no reason, or why you get headaches that seem to come out of nowhere, you're not alone. Millions of people are walking around with physical symptoms that don't seem to have a clear medical cause. The tests come back normal, but they still feel terrible.

What if I told you that your body might be trying to tell you something important? What if those mysterious aches and pains aren't signs that something is wrong with your organs, but signals that your nervous system doesn't feel safe?

Your body and your emotions aren't separate systems. They're so connected that scientists now talk about them as one integrated network. When your mind feels threatened, your body responds. When your body is under stress, it affects your emotions. This conversation between your brain and your body is happening every second of every day, mostly without you even noticing.

Let me introduce you to one of the most important parts of this conversation: your vagus nerve.

The vagus nerve is like the main highway between your brain and your body. It's actually the longest nerve in your body, starting in your brainstem and traveling down through your neck, chest, and abdomen, connecting to your heart, lungs, stomach, and other vital organs.

This nerve has one primary job: to help you figure out whether you're safe or in danger. It's constantly scanning your internal and external environment, looking for signs of threat or safety, and then telling your body how to respond.

When your vagus nerve senses safety, it activates what's called your parasympathetic nervous system. This is your "rest and digest" mode. Your heart rate slows down, your breathing deepens, your muscles relax, and your digestive system works properly. You feel calm, connected, and able to think clearly.

But when your vagus nerve detects danger, it can respond in different ways depending on how threatened you feel.

If the threat seems manageable, it activates your sympathetic nervous system. This is your fight-or-flight response. Your heart races, your breathing gets shallow, your muscles tense up, and your digestive system shuts down to save energy for dealing with the danger.

But if the threat feels overwhelming or inescapable, your vagus nerve might trigger a shutdown response. This is when people freeze, feel numb, or disconnect from their bodies. It's your nervous system's last-ditch effort to protect you by essentially playing dead until the danger passes.

Here's what's fascinating: your vagus nerve doesn't just respond to obvious dangers like being chased by a wild animal. It responds to any situation that your brain interprets as threatening, including social rejection, work stress, financial worry, or even critical thoughts about yourself.

And here's the crucial part: when your vagus nerve keeps getting signals that you're in danger, it starts to change how your body functions on a basic level.

Let's look at how this shows up in your physical health.

First, let's talk about tension headaches and neck pain. When your nervous system is on high alert, your body automatically assumes a protective posture. Your shoulders creep up toward your ears. Your jaw clenches. The muscles at the base of your skull tighten up as if you're bracing for impact.

This isn't something you're doing on purpose. It's an automatic response that happens when your brain thinks you need to be ready to fight or run. But when you spend hours or days in this protective posture, those muscles get exhausted and start to hurt.

That headache that starts at the base of your skull and wraps around your head? That's often your nervous system holding tension from feeling unsafe. Those knots in your shoulders that never seem to go away? That's your body staying ready for a threat that never comes.

Your digestive system is another place where safety concerns show up in obvious ways. Your gut has its own nervous system, sometimes called the "second brain," and it's directly connected to your emotional state through the vagus nerve.

When your brain perceives danger, it sends a message to your digestive system to slow down or stop working. This makes sense from a survival perspective. If you're being chased by a predator, your body doesn't want to waste energy digesting lunch. It wants all your resources focused on escaping.

But what happens when your brain thinks you're in danger all the time? Your digestive system never gets the signal that it's safe to work properly. Food sits in your stomach longer than it should. Your intestines don't move things along the way they're supposed to. You might get stomach aches, nausea, constipation, or diarrhea for no clear medical reason.

Many people with chronic anxiety develop what doctors call irritable bowel syndrome or IBS. The symptoms are real and uncomfortable, but often no physical cause can be found. That's because the problem isn't in their digestive organs. It's in the communication between their brain and their gut.

Chronic fatigue is another common way that feeling unsafe shows up in the body. Being hypervigilant is exhausting work. Your brain is constantly scanning for threats, your muscles are staying partially tensed, and your stress response system is running in the background all day long.

It's like having a computer with too many programs running at once. Eventually, the whole system starts to slow down and overheat. You wake up tired even after a full night's sleep because your nervous system never fully relaxed. You feel drained by activities that used to energize you because your body is spending so much energy just trying to keep you safe.

Sleep problems are incredibly common in people whose nervous systems don't feel safe. Sleep is a vulnerable state. When you're asleep, you can't watch for danger or protect yourself from threats. So if your brain doesn't trust that you're truly safe, it will resist going into the deep, restorative stages of sleep.

You might have trouble falling asleep because your mind keeps racing through all the things that could go wrong tomorrow. You might wake up multiple times during the night, scanning your environment for problems. You might sleep for eight hours but wake up feeling like you didn't rest at all because your nervous system never fully let go.

Your immune system also suffers when your body doesn't feel safe. Chronic stress hormones like cortisol suppress your immune function. This made sense for our ancestors, who needed all their energy focused on immediate survival. But when stress hormones stay elevated for months or years, your body becomes less able to fight off infections, heal from injuries, or protect you from illness.

People under chronic stress get sick more often and take longer to recover. They're more likely to develop autoimmune conditions, where the immune system starts attacking healthy tissue. They might notice that every little cold turns into a major illness, or that cuts and bruises take forever to heal.

Even your heart gets involved in this safety conversation. When you feel safe and calm, your heart rate has natural variability. It speeds up a little when you breathe in and slows down when you breathe out. This heart rate variability is actually a sign of a healthy, resilient nervous system.

But when you're chronically stressed or anxious, your heart rate becomes more rigid and less variable. Your heart might race for no apparent reason, or you might notice irregular heartbeats when you're worried about something. Again, medical tests might come back normal, but your heart is responding to signals from your nervous system about safety and threat.

Your breathing patterns also change when you don't feel safe. Shallow, rapid breathing is part of the fight-or-flight response. It's designed to get more oxygen to your muscles quickly so you can run or fight. But when you breathe this way all the time, it actually maintains your anxiety and keeps your nervous system activated.

Many people with chronic anxiety develop a habit of breathing only into the top part of their chest instead of using their full lungs. This sends a constant signal to their brain that they're in danger, which keeps the anxiety cycle going.

Your muscles hold emotional tension in predictable patterns. Anger often shows up as tightness in the jaw and shoulders. Fear tends to create tension in the chest and upper back. Sadness frequently causes tightness in the throat and chest. Anxiety often manifests as tension everywhere, like your whole body is braced for impact.

These patterns aren't just metaphorical. They're real, measurable changes in muscle tension that happen automatically when you experience certain emotions. Over time, these patterns can become so familiar that your muscles stay partially contracted even when you're not consciously feeling stressed.

For women, the connection between safety and physical symptoms has some unique aspects. Monthly hormonal changes can make all of these patterns more intense. In the week before your period, when progesterone levels drop, your nervous system becomes more sensitive to stress. Physical symptoms that are manageable most of the month might become overwhelming during this time.

Many women notice that their anxiety, headaches, digestive issues, and sleep problems get worse right before their period. This isn't weakness or imagination. It's your nervous system responding to real hormonal changes that affect how you process stress and perceive safety.

Birth control pills can also affect how your nervous system responds to stress. Some women find that hormonal birth control helps stabilize their mood and reduces anxiety. Others find that it makes them feel more anxious or emotionally flat. These differences probably have to do with how synthetic hormones interact with your individual stress response system.

Pregnancy and the postpartum period create their own unique challenges for the nervous system. During pregnancy, your body is already working overtime to create and support new life. Your stress response system becomes more sensitive to protect both you and your growing baby.

After birth, the dramatic drop in hormones combined with sleep deprivation and the stress of caring for a newborn can leave your nervous system completely overwhelmed. Many of the physical symptoms that new mothers experience, from headaches to digestive issues to extreme fatigue, are actually signs that their nervous system is struggling to cope with this major life transition.

Cultural pressures around body image can also create chronic threat states in women. If you've grown up believing that your worth depends on how you look, your nervous system might interpret weight gain, aging, or any perceived flaw as a threat to your survival. This can create chronic anxiety that shows up as all the physical symptoms we've been discussing.

The beauty industry and diet culture deliberately trigger threat responses to sell products. They teach women to see their natural bodies as problems that need to be fixed. This keeps many women in a constant state of vigilance about their appearance, which their nervous system experiences as a chronic threat.

Now, it's important to say that not all physical symptoms are caused by nervous system dysregulation. There are real medical conditions that need proper treatment from healthcare professionals. The key is learning to work with doctors who understand the connection between emotional and physical health.

If you're experiencing persistent physical symptoms, you should definitely get them checked out medically. But if your tests come back normal and your symptoms persist, it might be worth exploring whether your nervous system is trying to tell you something about safety.

When you do seek medical care, it helps to find providers who understand trauma and the mind-body connection. These doctors are more likely to take your symptoms seriously and work with you to address both physical and emotional aspects of your health.

You also have the right to advocate for yourself in medical settings. If a doctor dismisses your symptoms as "just stress" or "all in your head," you can ask for specific tests or seek a second opinion. Your symptoms are real, regardless of their cause, and you deserve to have them taken seriously.

Learning to listen to your body's safety signals is one of the most important skills you can develop. Your physical symptoms aren't random or meaningless. They're your body's way of communicating with you about how safe or threatened you feel in your current environment.

When you start to pay attention to these signals, you might notice patterns. Maybe your stomach hurts every Sunday night when you think about the work week ahead. Maybe your shoulders tense up whenever you're around certain people. Maybe you get headaches when you're trying to make difficult decisions.

These physical sensations are information. They're your body's early warning system, letting you know that something in your environment is activating your threat response. When you learn to recognize and respond to these signals, you can start to address the underlying safety concerns before they turn into chronic physical problems.

Your body is constantly communicating about safety. Learning to listen to and understand this communication is key to healing both your physical symptoms and your underlying anxiety. Your body isn't betraying you with these symptoms. It's trying to protect you the only way it knows how.

Chapter 5 : The Social Safety Trap - Why People Are Your Biggest Trigger

You can handle natural disasters, but a text from your boss at 8 PM sends you into panic. Here's why humans are our biggest threat.

Think about this for a moment. You could probably handle a power outage, a flat tire, or even a medical emergency with relative calm. But a friend doesn't text you back for six hours, and suddenly you're convinced they hate you. Your partner uses a slightly different tone of voice, and your heart starts racing. A coworker gives you a strange look in the hallway, and you spend the rest of the day wondering what you did wrong.

Why is it that we can face actual physical dangers with courage, but social situations can send us into complete meltdown? The answer lies deep in our evolutionary history and the way our brains are wired for survival.

For millions of years, humans survived by living in small tribes. Being accepted by your group wasn't just nice to have. It was literally a matter of life and death. If your tribe rejected you, you would be left alone in a dangerous world with no protection, no resources, and no help finding food or shelter. Banishment from the group was essentially a death sentence.

Your brain still carries this ancient programming. Even though being rejected by your friend or criticized by your boss won't actually kill you in the modern world, your nervous system responds as if it might. Social threats activate the same alarm systems in your brain that would fire if you were being chased by a predator.

This is why a critical comment can hurt more than a physical injury. This is why the fear of public speaking ranks higher than the fear of death for many people. This is why you can lose sleep over a social interaction that lasted five minutes but seemed to go wrong.

Your brain has specialized circuits that are constantly monitoring your social environment for signs of acceptance or rejection. Scientists call this process neuroception, which means perception that happens below the level of conscious awareness. You're not actively thinking about whether someone likes you or whether you fit in. Your nervous system is doing this scanning automatically, every second of every day.

When these circuits detect signs of social safety, like genuine smiles, warm eye contact, or inclusive body language, they send calming signals throughout your body. Your heart rate slows, your breathing deepens, and your muscles relax. You feel good, confident, and able to be yourself.

But when these same circuits pick up signs of social threat, like facial expressions that seem cold, voices that sound annoyed, or body language that feels rejecting, they trigger your stress response just as powerfully as a physical danger would.

The tricky part is that you're not just responding to what's actually happening. You're also responding to what you think might be happening, based on your past experiences and current insecurities. Your brain fills in gaps with assumptions, and those assumptions are often wrong.

Your friend doesn't respond to your text immediately, so you assume they're angry at you. Your boss seems distracted during your meeting, so you decide they're disappointed in your work. Someone doesn't laugh at your joke, so you conclude they think you're stupid.

These assumptions feel completely real because your nervous system is treating them as if they're facts. Your body starts producing stress hormones and preparing for social rejection, even though you have no actual evidence that rejection is coming.

There's another fascinating aspect of how our brains process social information. You have special cells called mirror neurons that automatically copy the emotional states of people around you. When someone smiles, your mirror neurons fire as if you're smiling too. When someone looks anxious, your nervous system starts to feel anxious as well.

This emotional contagion happens completely automatically. You can't turn it off. It's designed to help you understand what others are feeling so you can respond appropriately and maintain your place in the group.

But this also means you're constantly absorbing the emotional states of everyone around you. If you're in a room with anxious people, you'll start to feel anxious too, even if you have nothing to be anxious about. If you're around angry people, you'll start to feel activated and defensive, even if their anger has nothing to do with you.

Many sensitive people walk through the world like emotional sponges, soaking up everyone else's feelings and thinking those feelings are their own. They come home from work exhausted not because of what they did, but because of what they absorbed from their coworkers' stress, frustration, and anxiety.

The attachment patterns you developed in childhood play out powerfully in your adult relationships. If you learned as a child that love was unpredictable or conditional, your adult relationships might feel like constant tests that you might fail at any moment.

People with anxious attachment styles often become hypervigilant about their relationships. They analyze every text message for hidden meanings. They notice every subtle change in their partner's behavior and assume it means something bad. They need constant reassurance but then worry that asking for reassurance is pushing people away.

People with avoidant attachment styles often shut down when relationships start to feel too close or demanding. They might withdraw emotionally when their partner tries to discuss feelings. They might feel trapped by others' expectations and pull away to protect their independence.

People with disorganized attachment might swing between desperately wanting closeness and being terrified of it. They might pick fights to create distance when intimacy feels too scary, then panic when the other person actually backs away.

These patterns aren't conscious choices. They're automatic responses that your nervous system learned early and still uses to try to keep you safe in relationships.

Let's look at some specific ways that social threats show up in daily life.

Rejection sensitivity is when you're constantly on the look-out for signs that people might not want you around. You might interpret neutral expressions as disapproval. You might assume that invitations are given out of pity rather than genuine interest. You might avoid reaching out to people because you're so afraid of being turned down.

This hypersensitivity to rejection often becomes a self-fulfilling prophecy. When you're constantly expecting to be rejected, you might act in ways that actually push people away. You might be defensive when no defense is needed. You might withdraw before giving people a chance to get close. You might test relationships by creating drama to see if people will stick around.

Fear of abandonment can make people become people-pleasers who say yes to everything and never express their own needs or boundaries. They're so afraid of conflict that they'll sacrifice their own well-being to keep others happy.

But this strategy often backfires because relationships without boundaries aren't sustainable or genuine.

People-pleasing might look like kindness, but it's actually a fear response. You're not saying yes because you want to help. You're saying yes because you're afraid of what will happen if you say no. You're not being nice because you care about others. You're being nice because you need others to like you to feel safe.

Social comparison is another huge source of social threat in the modern world. You're not just comparing yourself to the people you actually know. Thanks to social media, you're comparing yourself to carefully curated highlight reels of thousands of strangers' lives.

Your brain doesn't understand that the perfect family photos you see online took fifty tries to get right. It doesn't know that the friend who seems to have an amazing social life is actually posting old photos to make herself look more popular. It just sees evidence that everyone else is happier, more successful, and more loved than you are.

This constant comparison activates your nervous system's threat response because your brain interprets being "less than" as a danger to your social survival. If you're not measuring up, maybe you'll be cast out of the group. If you're not successful enough, maybe you're not worthy of love and belonging.

For women, social safety threats have some unique aspects because of cultural messages about female worth and behavior. Women are often taught from childhood that their value depends on being liked and accepted by others. They learn to monitor others' reactions carefully and adjust their behavior to maintain approval.

This creates what researchers call a double bind. Women are criticized for being too much or too little of everything. Too aggressive or too passive. Too emotional or too cold. Too ambitious or too content. Too independent or too needy. No matter what choice you make, someone will have a problem with it.

This impossible standard keeps many women in a constant state of social anxiety. They're always second-guessing themselves, wondering if they said the right thing, wore the right outfit, or struck the right balance between all the competing expectations.

Female friendships can be particularly complex because women are often taught to compete with each other for male attention and social status, while also being expected to be supportive and collaborative. This can create relationships that feel simultaneously intimate and threatening.

Many women have experienced friendship betrayals that left deep scars on their ability to trust other women. They might have been excluded by a group, had secrets shared, or felt judged by people they thought were friends. These experiences can make adult female friendships feel risky and unstable.

In the workplace, women face additional challenges around social safety. They might worry about being seen as too emotional if they express feelings, but too cold if they don't. They might feel like they have to work twice as hard to prove themselves, but then worry about appearing threatening to male colleagues if they're too successful.

Imposter syndrome is often really social safety anxiety in disguise. The fear isn't just that you don't know what you're doing. It's that other people will discover you don't know what you're doing and reject you from the professional group you're trying to belong to.

Dating and sexual safety create their own unique social threats for women. The need to be attractive and desirable conflicts with the need to be safe and respected. Women have to navigate showing interest without seeming desperate, being friendly without leading someone on, and protecting themselves without seeming paranoid or rude.

The rise of online dating has made these dynamics even more complex. You're making split-second judgments about potential partners based on limited information, while they're doing the same to you. The abundance of choices can make everyone feel replaceable and disposable.

Social media has amplified all of these social safety concerns. You're not just managing your relationships with the people you see in person. You're managing your online presence, monitoring likes and comments, and comparing your real life to everyone else's highlight reel.

The constant availability that technology creates can make it feel like you're always on call for social obligations. You might feel anxiety if you don't respond to messages immediately, but also feel overwhelmed by the constant stream of social input. The fear of missing out competes with the need for downtime and solitude.

Online harassment is a real threat that affects many people, especially women, and can make the entire internet feel like a dangerous place. Even if you've never experienced severe online harassment yourself, knowing that it happens can make all your online interactions feel potentially threatening.

The paradox of digital connection is that you can feel simultaneously overwhelmed by social input and starved for real intimacy. You might have hundreds of online connections but feel deeply lonely. You might spend hours engaging with people on social media but feel like no one really knows you.

So how do you create social safety in a world that often feels socially threatening?

The first step is learning to recognize which relationships and social situations actually feel safe versus which ones trigger your threat response. Some people have a calming effect on your nervous system. After spending time with them, you feel more like yourself, more relaxed, and more confident. These are your safe people.

Other people, no matter how much you might care about them, seem to activate your stress response. You find yourself walking on eggshells around them, second-guessing your words, or feeling drained after interactions. This doesn't necessarily make them bad people, but it does make them unsafe for your nervous system.

Creating boundaries isn't about building walls to keep people out. It's about creating guidelines that help you stay regulated and authentic in your relationships. This might mean limiting time with people who consistently stress you out. It might mean being honest about your needs instead of automatically saying yes to everything. It might mean ending relationships that require you to be someone you're not.

You can't control how other people behave, but you can control how much access you give them to your energy and attention. You can choose to spend more time with people who support your nervous system regulation and less time with people who consistently trigger your threat response.

This isn't selfish. It's necessary for your mental and physical health. When you're regulated and feeling safe in your relationships, you have more to give to the people you care about. When you're constantly triggered and defensive, you're not showing up as your best self for anyone.

Learning to create social safety is one of the most important skills you can develop. Your relationships have the power to heal or harm your nervous system every single day. When you become conscious about choosing and cultivating relationships that support your wellbeing, you're giving yourself one of the greatest gifts possible: the experience of belonging without having to sacrifice who you are.

You can't control other people, but you can create social safety through boundaries and conscious relationship choices. This is how you begin to break free from the social safety trap that keeps so many people anxious, exhausted, and disconnected from their authentic selves.

Chapter 6 : The Perfectionist's Prison - How Excellence Became Your Enemy

The voice that drives you to excel is the same voice that never lets you rest. It's time to understand why perfectionism is your nervous system's attempt at safety.

If you've ever spent three hours writing an email that should have taken five minutes, you know what I'm talking about. If you've ever redone a project that was already good enough because it wasn't quite perfect, you understand this struggle. If you've ever lain awake at night replaying a conversation and criticizing yourself for not saying exactly the right thing, you're familiar with the prison of perfectionism.

Most people think perfectionism is about having high standards or caring about quality. But that's not what perfectionism really is. True perfectionism isn't about excellence. It's about fear. It's about trying to create safety by being so flawless that no one can criticize you, reject you, or find fault with you.

The perfectionist voice in your head isn't trying to help you succeed. It's trying to help you survive. It's your threat detection system working overtime, scanning for every possible mistake or flaw that might make you vulnerable to attack, rejection, or abandonment.

Here's what's happening in your brain when perfectionism takes over.

Your brain has a built-in error detection system that's designed to help you learn from mistakes and improve your performance. In healthy people, this system notices errors, feels a brief moment of discomfort, and then moves on to figuring out how to do better next time.

But in perfectionists, this error detection system becomes hyperactive. It's like having a smoke alarm that goes off when you burn toast. Every tiny mistake feels like a major catastrophe. Every small imperfection feels like evidence that you're fundamentally flawed or inadequate.

Brain scans of people with perfectionist tendencies show different patterns of activity in areas related to error monitoring and emotional regulation. When perfectionists make mistakes, their brains light up with activity in regions associated with threat detection and self-criticism. The emotional response to errors is much stronger and lasts much longer than it should.

At the same time, the reward system in perfectionist brains doesn't work the way it should. Normal brains feel

satisfaction and pleasure when they accomplish something well. But perfectionist brains focus so intensely on
what's wrong or what could be better that they rarely experience the reward of a job well done.

This creates a terrible cycle. You work incredibly hard to
achieve something, but instead of feeling proud or satis-
fied when you succeed, you immediately start focusing on
how it could have been better. Your brain never gets the
positive reinforcement that would make all that hard
work feel worthwhile.

There are different flavors of perfectionism, and understanding which type you struggle with can help you recognize it more clearly.

Self-oriented perfectionism is when you set impossible
standards for yourself. You believe that you must be perfect in everything you do, and anything less than perfection feels like failure. You might spend hours researching
the perfect gift for someone's birthday, or rewrite the
same paragraph twenty times because it doesn't sound
quite right.

Other-oriented perfectionism is when you expect everyone else to be perfect too. You get frustrated when people
don't meet your standards. You might feel annoyed when

your partner doesn't load the dishwasher exactly the way you would, or disappointed when friends don't put as much effort into plans as you do.

Socially prescribed perfectionism is when you believe that other people expect you to be perfect. You feel like you're constantly being judged and evaluated, and that any mistake or flaw will result in criticism or rejection. This type often develops in childhood when love and approval seemed conditional on being "good" or achieving certain standards.

All three types of perfectionism are rooted in the same basic fear: that imperfection equals danger. Your nervous system has learned to treat mistakes, flaws, and criticism as threats to your survival, even when logically you know they're not.

The perfectionism cycle works like this: You set standards that are impossibly high. Because no human can actually be perfect, you inevitably fall short of these standards. When you fail to meet your impossible expectations, you feel shame and self-criticism. To avoid feeling that shame again, you set even higher standards next time, convinced that if you just try harder or do better, you'll finally be safe from criticism and rejection.

But here's the cruel irony: perfectionism creates the very problems it's trying to solve. When you're constantly focused on avoiding mistakes, you become more likely to make them because you're anxious and overthinking everything. When you're terrified of criticism, you become more sensitive to it and more likely to interpret neutral feedback as an attack.

Perfectionism also makes you less likeable and harder to be around, which increases the risk of the rejection you're trying to avoid. People don't connect with perfection. They connect with authenticity, vulnerability, and shared struggles. When you present a perfect facade, you make it impossible for others to truly know and love the real you.

The exhaustion of perfectionism is real and profound. You're constantly scanning for errors, trying to anticipate problems, and pushing yourself to unrealistic standards. Your nervous system stays activated because there's always something that could be better, always another mistake to worry about making.

This chronic state of stress takes a toll on every aspect of your life. You might procrastinate on important projects because the fear of not doing them perfectly makes it too scary to start. You might avoid new opportunities because you're not confident you can excel immediately. You might miss deadlines because you're spending too much time perfecting work that was already good enough.

For women, perfectionism carries some unique challenges because of societal expectations and cultural messages about female worth and behavior.

Women are often expected to be perfect in multiple roles simultaneously. You're supposed to be a successful professional, a loving partner, a devoted mother, a good daughter, a supportive friend, and maintain a beautiful home and appearance while making it all look effortless. This "superwoman syndrome" sets women up for perfectionist anxiety from the start.

The message many girls receive growing up is that their worth depends on being pleasing, achieving, and never causing trouble. They learn that love and approval come from being "good girls" who excel in school, follow rules, and make others comfortable. This creates a deep association between perfection and safety that can last a lifetime.

Body perfectionism is particularly damaging for women because the cultural standards of female beauty are not only unrealistic but constantly changing. Women are taught to see their natural bodies as projects that need to be perfected through diet, exercise, makeup, clothing, and sometimes surgery. The time, energy, and mental space devoted to trying to achieve physical perfection is enormous and ultimately futile.

In professional settings, women often feel they need to be twice as good to get half the recognition. This pressure to prove themselves can fuel perfectionist tendencies that become exhausting and counterproductive. The fear of being seen as incompetent or unworthy can make women overwork, over-prepare, and second-guess their abilities constantly.

Motherhood brings its own perfectionist pressures. The cultural ideal of the "good mother" is someone who is endlessly patient, always puts her children's needs first, creates Pinterest-worthy experiences, and raises children who are well-behaved, high-achieving, and happy all the time. Real motherhood is messy, exhausting, and full of moments when you don't know what you're doing, but many mothers feel like admitting this makes them failures.

The hidden costs of perfectionism extend far beyond just feeling stressed or working too hard.

Chronic anxiety is almost inevitable when you're con-stantly trying to avoid any possibility of criticism or fail-ure. Your nervous system stays activated, always scanning for potential problems or mistakes. This creates physical symptoms like headaches, stomach issues, sleep prob-lems, and chronic tension.

Decision paralysis happens when the fear of making the wrong choice becomes so overwhelming that you can't make any choice at all. You might spend hours research-ing the best option for something simple like which res-taurant to go to or which brand of laundry detergent to buy.

Procrastination often goes hand-in-hand with perfection-ism because the fear of not doing something perfectly can make it feel too scary to start at all. You put off important tasks until the last minute, then rush through them in a panic, which ironically makes you more likely to make the mistakes you were trying to avoid.

Relationships suffer when perfectionism takes over. You might be critical of partners, friends, or family members who don't meet your standards. You might be afraid to show vulnerability or admit mistakes, which prevents real intimacy. You might avoid dating or close friendships because you're afraid people won't like you if they see your flaws.

Creativity becomes impossible when you're terrified of making something imperfect. Art, writing, music, and other creative pursuits require experimentation, play, and acceptance of mistakes as part of the learning process. Perfectionism kills creativity because it makes the creative process feel too risky.

Physical health suffers under the chronic stress of perfectionist anxiety. Your immune system becomes compromised. Your sleep is disrupted by racing thoughts about what you should have done better. Your digestive system struggles because you're always tense and worried.

The opportunity costs are huge. While you're spending three hours perfecting an email, you could be doing something that actually matters to you. While you're avoiding new challenges because you might not excel immediately, you're missing chances to learn and grow.

So how do you begin to break free from the perfectionist prison?

The first step is recognizing perfectionism for what it really is: a trauma response. Your nervous system learned early that mistakes were dangerous, that approval was conditional, and that being perfect was the only way to stay safe. This made sense given your early experiences, but it's not serving you now.

Start paying attention to your internal dialogue when you're working on something or facing a challenge. Notice when the perfectionist voice shows up. What does it say? How does it make your body feel? What emotions does it trigger?

Common perfectionist thoughts include: "This has to be perfect or people will think I'm incompetent." "If I make a mistake, everyone will see that I don't know what I'm doing." "I can't submit this until it's exactly right." "Other people will do this better than me."

These thoughts might feel true and rational, but they're actually fear-based assumptions that your nervous system is making to try to keep you safe.

Practice what I call "good enough" experiments. Deliberately do something at 80% of your usual standard and see what happens. Send the email after the second draft instead of the tenth. Submit the report that's well done but not perfect. Show up to the social gathering without spending two hours on your appearance.

Most of the time, you'll discover that your fears were unfounded. The email was fine. The report was well received. People were happy to see you regardless of how you looked. These experiences start to teach your nervous system that perfection isn't actually necessary for safety.

Reframe your relationship with mistakes and failures. Instead of seeing them as evidence of your inadequacy, try to see them as information. What can you learn from this experience? How can you use this feedback to improve next time? What would you tell a good friend who had the same experience?

Develop a self-compassion practice to counter the harsh self-criticism that fuels perfectionism. When you notice yourself being self-critical, pause and ask: "What do I need right now? How can I be kind to myself in this moment? What would I say to someone I loved who was struggling with this?"

Remember that perfectionism is not the same as having high standards or caring about quality. You can still do excellent work and pursue meaningful goals without demanding flawless performance from yourself. Excellence with self-compassion is sustainable. Perfectionism is not.

The goal isn't to become careless or stop caring about doing good work. The goal is to find the middle ground where you can pursue excellence without sacrificing your mental health, relationships, and well-being in the process.

Perfectionism promises safety but delivers anxiety. It promises acceptance but creates isolation. It promises success but often leads to paralysis and missed opportunities. Breaking free from the perfectionist prison isn't about lowering your standards. It's about raising your standards for how you treat yourself and what you're willing to sacrifice in the pursuit of an impossible ideal.

You are worthy of love and belonging exactly as you are, flaws and all. Your worth doesn't depend on perfect performance. Your safety doesn't require flawless execution. The voice that drives you to excel can learn to be encouraging rather than demanding, supportive rather than critical. This is how you transform excellence from an enemy back into an ally.

Chapter 7 : The Modern Mind Trap - How Technology Hijacked Your Safety System

Every ping, buzz, and notification is a tiny shot of adrenaline. Your phone isn't just distracting you - it's training your brain to be anxious.

Picture this: You're trying to relax on a Sunday afternoon, maybe reading a book or having a quiet conversation. Suddenly your phone buzzes. Without even thinking about it, your heart rate jumps a little. Your attention immediately shifts to the phone. Your mind starts wondering what the notification might be. Is it important? Is someone trying to reach you? Are you missing something?

That small jolt you feel every time your phone makes a sound isn't just annoyance. It's your ancient alarm system responding to what it perceives as a potential threat. Your brain doesn't understand the difference between a text message and a predator approaching your cave. It just knows that something unexpected happened, and in the world your nervous system evolved for, unexpected things were often dangerous.

Now multiply that experience by the hundreds of notifications most people receive every day. Each ping is training your nervous system to be on high alert. Each buzz is teaching your brain that relaxation is dangerous because you might miss something important. Each notification is reinforcing the idea that you need to be constantly vigilant to stay safe.

The companies that create our phones, apps, and social media platforms understand this better than most of us do. They employ teams of neuroscientists, behavioral economists, and addiction specialists whose job is to make their products as compelling and hard to put down as possible. They're not just trying to get your attention. They're trying to hijack your brain's reward and threat detection systems to keep you coming back for more.

Here's how they do it.

Your brain has a chemical called dopamine that gets released when you experience or anticipate something rewarding. Dopamine isn't actually the pleasure chemical, like many people think. It's the anticipation chemical. It gets released when your brain thinks something good might be about to happen.

In the natural world, dopamine helped our ancestors survive by motivating them to seek out food, shelter, and mates. When they saw signs that food might be nearby,

dopamine would give them the energy and focus to go
find it.

Technology companies have figured out how to trigger
this same system with notifications, likes, comments, and
other digital rewards. But here's the key: they don't give
you rewards on a predictable schedule. Instead, they use
what psychologists call intermittent reinforcement.

Sometimes when you check your phone, there's something interesting waiting for you. Sometimes there's nothing. Sometimes there's something amazing that makes
you feel great. This unpredictability is what makes the behavior so addictive. Your brain keeps hoping that this
time, there might be something good waiting.

It's the same principle that makes gambling so compelling. You never know when you might hit the jackpot, so
you keep pulling the lever. Every time you pick up your
phone, you're essentially pulling a slot machine lever,
hoping for a social or informational reward.

This creates what researchers call continuous partial attention. You're never fully focused on any one thing because part of your mind is always monitoring for digital
input. You might be having a conversation with someone
you love, but you're also half-listening for notification

sounds. You might be working on an important project, but you're also wondering if there are new messages waiting.

This state of divided attention is exhausting for your nervous system. It never gets to fully relax because it's always monitoring multiple streams of potential information. It's like trying to watch three movies at once. You might catch pieces of each one, but you can't really enjoy or fully understand any of them.

The constant connectivity also means that your brain never gets a break from social input. In the past, when you came home from work or social activities, you could truly disconnect and recharge. Now, your friends, family, coworkers, and even strangers can reach you anytime through texts, emails, social media, and a dozen other platforms.

Your nervous system doesn't understand that these digital interactions aren't the same as face-to-face ones. When someone sends you an angry email, your brain responds with the same stress hormones it would release if that person were yelling at you in person. When you see social media posts that make you feel excluded or inadequate, your nervous system reacts as if you were actually being rejected by your social group.

Social media platforms are particularly skillful at exploiting your brain's social survival instincts. They've turned normal human activities like sharing experiences and seeking approval into a competitive game where everyone is constantly comparing themselves to everyone else.

Every photo you see of someone's vacation, every announcement of their achievements, every glimpse into their seemingly perfect relationships becomes a potential threat to your social standing. Your brain starts asking: "Why isn't my life that exciting? Why don't I look that happy? Why aren't my relationships that perfect?"

The problem is that you're not comparing your real life to other people's real lives. You're comparing your messy, complicated, behind-the-scenes reality to other people's carefully curated highlight reels. It's like comparing how you look when you first wake up to how celebrities look on the red carpet after three hours with professional hair and makeup artists.

But your nervous system doesn't know that. It just sees evidence that everyone else is happier, more successful, and more loved than you are. This activates your threat detection system because in ancient times, being at the bottom of the social hierarchy was genuinely dangerous.

The blue light that screens emit creates additional problems for your nervous system. Your brain uses natural light cycles to regulate your internal clock and stress hormones. When you expose yourself to bright blue light late in the evening, you're telling your brain that it's still daytime and it needs to stay alert.

This disrupts your sleep, which makes your nervous system more reactive and less able to handle stress during the day. Poor sleep also interferes with your brain's ability to process emotions and consolidate memories, which can make you feel more anxious and overwhelmed.

Many people now experience something called nomophobia, which is the fear of being without your mobile phone. The anxiety that people feel when they can't check their devices isn't just psychological dependence. It's their nervous system genuinely perceiving disconnection as a threat.

There's also phantom vibration syndrome, where people feel their phone vibrating even when it's not. This happens because your nervous system has become so hypervigilant about missing notifications that it starts creating false alarms. Your brain is so primed to detect phone signals that it interprets other sensations as vibrations that aren't there.

For women, the digital world creates some unique safety challenges. Social media platforms tend to amplify appearance-based comparisons and body image pressures. The endless stream of filtered photos, beauty tutorials, and diet advice can make women feel like they're constantly being evaluated and found lacking.

Online harassment patterns also disproportionately affect women, especially women of color, LGBTQ+ women, and women in public positions. The threat of receiving cruel comments, unwanted sexual attention, or even doxxing and stalking can make the entire internet feel like a dangerous place.

Dating apps have turned romantic relationships into a marketplace where people swipe through potential partners like they're shopping online. This commodification of human connection can make dating feel dehumanizing and trigger fears about being rejected based on superficial criteria.

The pressure of maintaining digital personas adds another layer of stress for many women. There's the expectation to post regularly, to look perfect in photos, to seem happy and successful all the time, and to engage with others' content in socially appropriate ways. This digital emotional labor can be exhausting and anxiety-provoking.

Information overload is another way that technology overwhelms our nervous systems. We now have access to more information in a single day than our ancestors encountered in their entire lifetimes. Our brains, which evolved to handle local, relevant information, are trying to process global news, expert opinions, scientific studies, political debates, and social commentary from around the world.

The 24-hour news cycle deliberately uses threat-based language and imagery to capture attention. Stories are framed to trigger your survival instincts: "This common household item could kill you." "New study reveals shocking danger in everyday activity." "Local crime wave has residents terrified."

Your brain doesn't understand that most of this information isn't personally relevant to your safety. It just processes the emotional tone and assumes that if there's this much talk about danger, you must be in a dangerous world. This creates a chronic state of background anxiety that can make everything else feel more threatening.

The negativity bias in media means you're exposed to far more information about problems, dangers, and conflicts than about positive developments or normal, peaceful activities. This skews your perception of reality and makes the world seem more dangerous than it actually is.

Decision fatigue is another hidden cost of our digital world. Every day, you're faced with thousands of micro-choices: which articles to read, which posts to like, which messages to respond to, which videos to watch. Your brain uses the same energy to make these small decisions as it does for important ones, leaving you mentally exhausted.

The abundance of choice in everything from restaurants to romantic partners can create what psychologists call the paradox of choice. When you have too many options, decision-making becomes overwhelming rather than liberating. You might spend more time choosing what to watch on Netflix than actually watching anything.

So how do you protect your nervous system from digital overwhelm while still benefiting from technology's genuine advantages?

The first step is recognizing that your phone and other devices are designed to capture and hold your attention in ways that can be harmful to your mental health. This isn't a personal failing or lack of willpower. It's your brain responding normally to tools that are deliberately engineered to be irresistible.

Start by becoming aware of how technology affects your nervous system. Notice what happens in your body when you get a notification. Pay attention to how you feel after spending time on social media. Observe how your sleep and stress levels change when you use screens late at night.

Create intentional boundaries around your technology use. This might mean turning off non-essential notifications, putting your phone in another room while you sleep, or designating certain times of day as phone-free zones.

Consider implementing regular digital detox periods, whether that's a few hours each day, one day per week, or longer breaks when you need them. Use this time to engage in activities that calm your nervous system, like spending time in nature, reading physical books, or having face-to-face conversations.

When you do use social media, try to consume it mindfully rather than scrolling mindlessly. Ask yourself: "How is this making me feel? Is this information helpful or harmful to my wellbeing? Am I using this tool, or is it using me?"

Replace some digital activities with analog alternatives that support nervous system regulation. Instead of reading news on your phone first thing in the morning, try starting your day with meditation, journaling, or gentle movement. Instead of scrolling through social media when you're bored, try calling a friend, taking a walk, or engaging in a creative hobby.

Create physical spaces in your home that are free from technology. This gives your nervous system a place to truly rest and recharge without the constant possibility of digital input.

Remember that technology itself isn't evil or harmful. It's a tool that can be used in ways that support your wellbeing or undermine it. The key is becoming conscious about how you use it and making choices that serve your mental health rather than sabotaging it.

Your nervous system evolved to handle the challenges of a much simpler world. It's not your fault that modern technology can overwhelm and dysregulate you. But it is your responsibility to learn how to protect yourself from its potentially harmful effects while still enjoying its genuine benefits.

Technology can be a tool for connection and growth, but conscious use is essential for maintaining nervous system health. When you take control of your digital environment instead of letting it control you, you're taking an important step toward creating the safety and calm that your brain has been seeking all along.

Chapter 8 : The Inherited Anxiety - Breaking Generational Cycles of Fear

Your grandmother's unspoken fears live in your DNA. Your mother's anxiety patterns echo in your nervous system. It's time to break the chain.

Sarah sits in her therapist's office, crying about her fear of money running out. She has a good job, savings in the bank, and no real financial problems. But every night, she lies awake worrying about becoming homeless. "I don't understand why I feel this way," she says. "My life is nothing like my grandmother's." But that's exactly the point. Sarah's grandmother lived through the Great Depression, when families lost everything overnight. That fear of not having enough never left her. She passed it to Sarah's mother, who hoarded coupons and worried about every penny. Now Sarah carries the same fear, even though she's never known real hunger or homelessness.

This is how anxiety travels through families. It moves from parent to child like a secret message written in invisible ink. The child doesn't know they're carrying it, but it shows up in their body, their thoughts, and their choices. Scientists now know that trauma and stress don't just affect the person who lived through them. They can actually change how genes work, and these changes can be passed down to children and grandchildren.

Think of your genes like a piano. The keys are always there, but which songs get played depends on what's happening around the piano. When someone goes through trauma or long periods of stress, it's like certain keys get stuck or others get played too often. These patterns can be passed down, so the child's piano starts playing similar songs, even if they never learned the music.

Researchers have studied the children and grandchildren of Holocaust survivors. Many of these younger generations show signs of trauma responses, even though they never experienced the Holocaust themselves. Their nervous systems seem to be set to high alert, always watching for danger that their grandparents faced decades ago. The same patterns show up in families affected by war, poverty, and other major stresses.

But genes are only part of the story. Children also learn anxiety by watching their parents. A toddler doesn't know that the world is safe or dangerous on their own. They look to their caregivers' faces and bodies for clues. If mom jumps every time the phone rings, the child learns that phones might bring bad news. If dad checks the locks three times before bed, the child learns that the world is full of threats trying to get in.

Families often organize themselves around anxiety like planets orbiting the sun. One person might become the worrier who thinks about all the things that could go wrong. Another becomes the fixer who tries to solve every problem. Someone else might become the distractor who makes jokes when things get tense. These roles feel natural, but they're actually the family's way of managing fear together.

Maria grew up in a family where her mother worried about everything. Every cough meant pneumonia. Every late arrival meant a car accident. Maria learned to call home every few hours to calm her mother's fears. Now, as an adult, Maria can't enjoy a vacation without constantly texting her own children to make sure they're safe. She's become the family worrier, just like her mother before her.

Money anxiety is one of the most common patterns passed down through generations. Families who lived through poverty, job loss, or financial instability often develop beliefs that there's never enough. Children in these families might hear phrases like "money doesn't grow on trees" or "we can't afford that" so often that they grow up believing financial security is impossible. Even when these children become successful adults, they might still feel anxious about spending money on anything that isn't absolutely necessary.

Health anxiety also travels through family lines. Parents who lived through serious illness or who lost loved ones to disease often become hypervigilant about symptoms. They might rush to the doctor for every headache or worry that fatigue means something terrible. Children learn that bodies are fragile and dangerous. They grow up scanning their own bodies for signs of illness, turning normal sensations into sources of fear.

Relationship patterns pass from parent to child like family recipes. Children who watched their parents fight learn that love includes conflict. Those who saw a parent leave learn that people you love will abandon you. Children whose parents stayed in unhappy marriages might learn that commitment means suffering. These early lessons about love and safety shape how they approach relationships as adults.

Women often carry extra weight when it comes to family anxiety. In many cultures, women are expected to be the emotional caretakers of the family. They're the ones who worry about everyone's feelings, remember important dates, and make sure family relationships stay strong. Mothers often feel responsible not just for their own anxiety, but for managing everyone else's emotions too.

The relationship between mothers and daughters can be especially intense when it comes to passing down anxiety. Mothers often project their own fears about the world onto their daughters. A mother who experienced sexual assault might become overprotective, warning her daughter about the dangers of being female. A mother who struggled with body image might make comments about her daughter's appearance, trying to protect her from the same pain but actually passing on the same fears.

Cultural expectations about women's roles add another layer of inherited anxiety. For generations, women had little power over their own lives. They couldn't vote, own property, or make decisions about their own bodies. This powerlessness created anxiety about safety and security that still echoes in modern women. Even though legal and social changes have given women more freedom, the nervous system patterns of hypervigilance and fear can persist.

Historical trauma affects entire communities, not just individual families. Native American communities still carry the trauma of forced relocation and cultural destruction. African American families carry the intergenerational effects of slavery and ongoing discrimination. Immigrant families often carry anxiety about belonging and safety that started with the dangerous journey to a new country.

These community-wide trauma patterns create shared ways of seeing the world. Children grow up learning not just from their own families, but from their neighbors, teachers, and community leaders who all carry similar fears. The anxiety becomes woven into the culture itself, showing up in stories, warnings, and unspoken rules about how to stay safe.

But here's what's remarkable about being human: we have the power to change these patterns. Understanding that your anxiety might not even be yours is the first step toward freedom. When you recognize that the voice in your head warning you about disaster sounds just like your mother's voice, you can start to question whether those warnings are really necessary for your life.

Breaking generational cycles starts with mapping your family's anxiety patterns. Think about the messages you received growing up about safety, money, relationships, and health. What did your parents worry about most? What stories did they tell about their own childhoods? What warnings did they give you about the world?

Notice which of your fears seem too big for your actual life experiences. If you're terrified of poverty but you've never been poor, that fear might belong to someone else in your family tree. If you can't relax in relationships despite having loving partners, you might be carrying someone else's heartbreak.

The goal isn't to blame your parents or grandparents for passing on their fears. They were doing their best to protect you with the tools they had. Their anxiety often came from real dangers they faced. Your grandmother's fear of running out of food made sense if she lived through times when food was scarce. Your father's distrust of authority might have kept him safe in situations where authority figures were actually dangerous.

Healing generational trauma means honoring your family's survival while choosing different patterns for yourself. You can be grateful that your grandmother's vigilance helped her survive difficult times while deciding that level of vigilance isn't necessary in your current life. You can appreciate that your parents' anxiety came from love while choosing to express love in less fearful ways.

One powerful technique for healing generational patterns is visualization work with your ancestors. Imagine sitting with your grandmother, mother, and other important family members. Thank them for their strength and survival. Acknowledge the fears they carried and how those fears helped them navigate real dangers. Then gently explain that you're safe now in ways they weren't, and that you're going to try a different approach.

Creating new family stories is another important part of breaking cycles. Instead of focusing on all the things that could go wrong, start telling stories about resilience, growth, and possibility. When you catch yourself passing on anxious warnings to children in your life, pause and ask whether there's a way to teach safety without teaching fear.

If you have children, conscious parenting means being aware of your own anxiety patterns so you don't automatically pass them on. This doesn't mean pretending you never worry or that the world has no dangers. It means processing your own fears in healthy ways so they don't spill over onto your children. It means teaching children to be appropriately careful without making them afraid of life itself.

Remember that children are always watching and learning from your nervous system, not just your words. If you tell them everything is fine while your body is tense and anxious, they'll learn to mistrust their own sense of safety. If you model healthy ways of dealing with stress and uncertainty, they'll internalize those patterns instead of anxiety patterns.

Sometimes breaking generational cycles means seeking therapy or other professional help. A skilled therapist can help you separate your own experiences from inherited trauma.

They can teach you techniques for calming your nervous system and creating new patterns of thinking and feeling. There's no shame in getting help to heal patterns that have been in your family for generations.

Community healing approaches can also be powerful for addressing cultural and historical trauma. Support groups, cultural ceremonies, and community education programs help people understand that their individual anxiety is part of larger patterns that affect many people. When entire communities work together to heal, the changes can be even more profound than individual healing alone.

As you work to break anxiety cycles in your own life, you become what therapists call a "cycle breaker." This is a powerful role that requires courage and commitment, but it's also deeply meaningful.

When you heal your own patterns, you don't just change your life – you change the trajectory for future generations.

Your children, and their children, will inherit your healing instead of your fear. They'll grow up with nervous systems that know how to be calm, minds that can imagine positive futures, and hearts that trust in their own ability to handle life's challenges. This is perhaps the most important gift you can give to the future.

The chain of inherited anxiety ends with you. Your grandmother's fears served their purpose – they kept her alive in dangerous times.

Your mother's worry showed her love in the only way she knew how. Now it's your turn to love yourself and future generations in a new way, with trust instead of fear, with calm instead of worry, with hope instead of dread. You have the power to transform generations of anxiety into a legacy of peace.

Chapter 9 : The Nervous System Reset - Practical Tools for Rewiring Your Safety Response

Your brain has been practicing anxiety for years. Now it's time to practice calm with the same dedication.

Lisa spent twenty years jumping at sudden sounds, scanning rooms for exits, and feeling her heart race at the smallest unexpected events. Her nervous system had become like a car alarm that goes off when a leaf touches it. Everything felt like a threat. But here's what she discovered that changed everything: just like her brain had learned to be anxious through practice, it could learn to be calm through practice too.

Your nervous system is like a highway system in your body. When you feel safe, traffic flows smoothly on calm, easy roads. When you feel threatened, all the traffic gets diverted to the emergency highways that make your heart pound and your muscles tense. The problem is that many of us have been living on those emergency highways for so long that our nervous system has forgotten how to use the calm roads.

Understanding how your nervous system works is like getting a map of those highways. There are three main states your nervous system can be in, and knowing which one you're in helps you choose the right tools to get back to safety.

The first state is what scientists call sympathetic activation, but you can think of it as your action state. This is when your body gets ready to fight or run away from danger. Your heart beats faster, your breathing gets shallow, your muscles tense up, and your mind starts racing. This state is perfect when you actually need to respond to real danger, like jumping out of the way of a car. But when your nervous system gets stuck here because of anxiety, you feel wired, restless, and like you can't slow down even when you're safe.

The second state is parasympathetic activation, or your rest state. This is when your body knows it's safe to relax, digest food, heal, and connect with others. Your heart rate slows down, your breathing deepens, your muscles soften, and your mind can be present and peaceful. This is where you want to spend most of your time when you're not facing real danger.

The third state is called dorsal vagal shutdown, but you can think of it as your collapse state. This happens when your nervous system decides that fighting or running won't work, so it shuts down instead. You might feel numb, disconnected, foggy, or like you're watching your life from outside your body. People in this state often say they feel like robots going through the motions or like they're living behind a thick wall of glass.

Your window of tolerance is like the zone where you can handle stress without getting pushed into panic or shutdown. Some people have a wide window and can deal with a lot of stress before getting overwhelmed. Others have a narrow window and small stresses push them into fight, flight, or freeze. The good news is that you can make your window wider through practice.

Breathing is one of the fastest ways to change your nervous system state because it's something you can control that directly affects your body's stress response. Your breath is like a remote control for your nervous system, and different breathing patterns send different messages to your brain about whether you're safe or in danger.

Box breathing is perfect when your mind is racing and you need to feel more grounded. Breathe in for four counts, hold for four counts, breathe out for four counts, and hold empty for four counts. Imagine drawing a box with your breath. This technique helps balance your nervous system and brings you back into your window of tolerance.

When you need to activate your rest state, try extended exhale breathing. Breathe in for four counts, then breathe out for eight counts. The long exhale tells your nervous system that you're safe enough to slow down. You can do this anywhere – in your car, at your desk, or lying in bed.

Coherent breathing helps your heart and brain work together more smoothly. Breathe in for five counts and out for five counts, making your breathing smooth and even like gentle waves. This creates something called heart rate variability, which is a sign of a healthy, flexible nervous system.

Your vagus nerve is like the main cable that carries calm signals from your brain to your body. You can activate it through humming, singing, or even gargling with water. The vibrations stimulate the nerve and help your body remember how to relax. This is why people often feel better after singing in the car or humming while they work.

Your body holds the memory of every stress and trauma you've experienced, but it also has the wisdom to heal itself when you give it the right tools. Progressive muscle relaxation helps you reconnect with your body in a safe way. Start with your toes and slowly tense each muscle group for five seconds, then release and notice how relaxation feels different from tension. Work your way up to your head, paying attention to the contrast between tight and loose muscles.

Self-massage is like giving your nervous system a gentle reminder that touch can be safe and healing. Use your hands to gently massage your temples, the base of your skull, your shoulders, or anywhere that holds tension. Even just placing your hands on your heart or belly can send calming signals to your brain.

Movement is medicine for an anxious nervous system, but it needs to be the right kind of movement. Gentle walking, especially in nature, helps discharge stress energy without overwhelming your system. Yoga that focuses on slow, mindful movements teaches your body that it can be strong and relaxed at the same time. Dancing, even just swaying to music in your living room, helps your body remember that movement can be joyful instead of just about escaping danger.

Your thoughts and your nervous system are constantly talking to each other. Anxious thoughts create physical stress, and physical tension creates more anxious thoughts. Breaking this cycle requires working with both your mind and body at the same time.

When you notice anxious thoughts, try getting curious about them instead of fighting them. Ask yourself: "Is this thought helpful right now? Is this worry about something happening now or something that might happen? What would I tell a good friend who had this thought?" This creates some space between you and the anxiety instead of getting completely tangled up in it.

Grounding techniques use your five senses to bring you back to the present moment when anxiety tries to pull you into scary future scenarios. Notice five things you can see, four things you can touch, three things you can hear, two things you can smell, and one thing you can taste. This simple exercise reminds your nervous system that you're here, now, and safe in this moment.

Women's nervous systems have some unique patterns that are important to understand. Your menstrual cycle affects how sensitive your nervous system is to stress. Many women notice they feel more anxious or over-whelmed during certain parts of their cycle. This isn't weakness – it's your body being honest about what it needs. During more sensitive times, you might need extra sleep, gentler exercise, and more nervous system support.

Body image anxiety is something many women carry, and it affects nervous system regulation in powerful ways. When you're constantly worried about how you look, your nervous system stays partially activated, always on guard against judgment or rejection. Practices that help you feel at home in your body, like gentle stretching or mindful eating, can help calm this particular type of vigilance.

Relationships can be both triggers and healing resources for women's nervous systems. Many women have learned to monitor other people's emotions constantly, which keeps the nervous system in a state of hyperalertness. Learning to notice when you're taking on someone else's stress and practicing ways to stay connected to your own experience is crucial for nervous system health.

Workplace anxiety affects many women differently than men because of additional pressures around being liked, being perfect, and managing other people's emotions while trying to do their jobs. Quick reset techniques that you can do at your desk, like putting your hand on your heart and taking three deep breaths, can help you stay regulated throughout the work day.

For deeper healing, there are advanced techniques that work with how trauma and stress get stored in your brain and body. Bilateral stimulation involves crossing the midline of your body to help both sides of your brain work together better. You can tap your hands alternately on your thighs, cross your arms and pat your shoulders, or even just march in place while focusing on a stressful memory until it feels less intense.

Internal Family Systems recognizes that we all have different parts of ourselves – the part that worries, the part that tries to be perfect, the part that wants to hide, and the part that knows how to be calm and wise. Instead of fighting the anxious parts, you can learn to listen to what they're trying to protect you from and help them relax by showing them that you can handle things now.

Creating your personal nervous system toolkit means having practices ready for different times of day and different levels of stress. Your morning practice might include five minutes of deep breathing and setting an intention for the day. Your midday reset could be a brief walk or some shoulder rolls at your desk. Your evening practice might involve gentle stretching and reflecting on three good things that happened during the day.

For emergency situations when anxiety hits hard and fast, you need tools that work quickly. The 5-4-3-2-1 grounding technique, cold water on your wrists, or even just naming your experience out loud ("I notice I'm feeling anxious right now, and that's okay") can help bring you back into your window of tolerance.

Safety anchors are internal resources you can create and strengthen over time. Think of a time when you felt completely safe and loved. It might be a memory of being hugged by a grandparent, sitting by a peaceful lake, or holding a pet. Practice bringing this memory to mind in vivid detail – what you saw, heard, felt, and smelled. The more you practice accessing this feeling of safety, the easier it becomes to find it when you need it.

Tracking your progress helps you notice improvements that might be so gradual you miss them otherwise. You might keep a simple daily rating of your overall nervous system state from one to ten, or notice patterns like how well you slept, how many times you felt overwhelmed, or how quickly you were able to calm down after feeling triggered.

Your nervous system has been protecting you in the only way it knew how, by staying alert for danger. This has probably served you in important ways, keeping you safe and helping you survive difficult experiences. Now you're teaching it that there are other options, that it can relax without letting its guard down completely, that safety is possible even in an uncertain world.

This rewiring doesn't happen overnight. Your nervous system learned its current patterns over months or years, and it will take time to learn new ones. But every moment you spend practicing regulation, every breath you take to calm yourself, every time you choose a grounding technique over spiraling into worry, you're literally changing your brain and nervous system.

The beautiful thing about nervous system healing is that it builds on itself. The calmer you become, the easier it is to stay calm. The more you practice feeling safe, the more natural safety begins to feel. Your nervous system starts to trust that you know how to take care of it, and it can finally start to rest after being on high alert for so long. This is how you reclaim your birthright of peace, one regulated breath at a time.

Chapter 10: Building Your Safety-First Life - Creating Environments Where You Can Thrive

Safety isn't just a feeling - it's a lifestyle. Here's how to architect a life that supports your nervous system's healing.

You've learned so much about your nervous system, how trauma affects your body and mind, and the tools that help you heal. Now comes the most important part - creating a life that supports all this hard work you've been doing. Think of this as building a house where your healed self can live comfortably.

Your nervous system has been working overtime for years, maybe decades. It's been scanning for danger, preparing for threats, and keeping you alive in the best way it knew how. Now that you understand how it works, you can create a world around you that helps it finally relax and trust that you're truly safe.

The spaces where you spend your time have a huge impact on how your nervous system feels. Your brain is constantly taking in information from your surroundings - the colors on the walls, the sounds in the room, how cluttered or organized things are, even the smell in the air. All of this information gets processed by your nervous system, which then decides if you're safe or if it needs to be on guard.

Start with your bedroom since this is where you rest and restore. Your bedroom should feel like a sanctuary - a place where your nervous system can truly let down its guard. This doesn't mean you need expensive furniture or perfect decorating. It means creating a space that feels peaceful to you. Maybe that's soft lighting instead of harsh overhead lights. Maybe it's keeping the room clean and organized so your brain doesn't have to process clutter. Maybe it's having plants that connect you to nature or photos that make you smile.

Think about what makes you feel calm. Some people need complete silence to relax, while others feel better with soft background noise. Some people love bright colors that make them happy, while others need neutral tones to feel peaceful. There's no right or wrong way to create your safe space - only what works for your unique nervous system.

Your workspace matters too, whether that's an office, your kitchen table, or wherever you do your daily tasks. If possible, add elements that help you stay regulated during stressful moments. This might be a small plant, a photo that makes you smile, or even just keeping the area organized so your brain can focus better. If you can't change much about your workspace, you can still bring small items that help you feel grounded - a smooth stone to hold when you're stressed, essential oil on a bracelet, or a picture that reminds you of your strength.

Light affects your nervous system more than you might realize. Harsh fluorescent lights can keep your system activated, while natural light helps regulate your daily rhythms. Try to get some natural light every day, especially in the morning. In the evening, dimmer lights help signal to your nervous system that it's time to start winding down.

Sound is another big factor. If you live in a noisy area, consider getting a white noise machine or playing soft background sounds that help mask sudden noises that might startle your system. If you're sensitive to sounds, noise-canceling headphones or earplugs can be lifesavers.

Don't forget about bringing nature inside. Plants, natural materials like wood and stone, or even pictures of nature can help your nervous system remember that the world isn't all concrete and stress. Your brain is wired to find nature calming, so even small touches of the natural world can make a difference.

The people in your life have the biggest impact on whether your nervous system feels safe or activated. Healthy relationships are like medicine for trauma - they show your nervous system that connection can be safe and nourishing. But unhealthy relationships can keep you stuck in survival mode, no matter how much other healing work you do.

Safe relationships have certain qualities. The people in them listen to you without trying to fix or judge you. They respect your boundaries and don't pressure you to do things that don't feel right. They're consistent - you can predict how they'll treat you from day to day. They support your healing journey instead of making you feel bad about your struggles.

This doesn't mean safe people are perfect or never have bad days. It means they take responsibility for their actions, they communicate directly instead of playing games, and they care about how their behavior affects you.

Learning to recognize safe people takes time, especially if you grew up around unsafe relationships. Your nervous system might have learned to mistake intensity for love, or chaos for normal. It's okay if it takes a while to trust your instincts about people. Start small - notice how you feel in your body when you're around different people. Do you feel relaxed and like yourself, or do you feel like you need to be on guard?

Setting boundaries is crucial for maintaining safety in relationships. Boundaries aren't walls that keep people out - they're guidelines that help relationships work better. When you set a boundary, you're teaching people how to treat you in a way that helps your nervous system stay regulated.

Good boundaries are clear and specific. Instead of saying "don't be mean to me," you might say "I need you to speak to me respectfully, without yelling or name-calling." Instead of feeling guilty about having needs, remember that healthy people want to treat you well - they just need to know what that looks like for you.

Sometimes you'll need to limit contact with people who consistently activate your nervous system, even if they're family members. This doesn't make you a bad person. You're not responsible for fixing other people or accepting treatment that hurts your healing. You can love someone and still choose to protect your peace.

Build a support network of people who understand trauma and healing. This might include friends who are also on healing journeys, support groups, online communities, or professional helpers like therapists. Having people who truly get what you're going through makes the journey less lonely and gives your nervous system evidence that you're not alone in this world.

Your daily routine and life choices can either support your nervous system's healing or keep it activated. Creating a lifestyle that supports your wellbeing isn't selfish - it's necessary medicine for your healing.

Start with your daily routine. Your nervous system loves predictability because it helps your brain know what to expect. This doesn't mean your days have to be boring or exactly the same. It means having some consistent elements that help you feel grounded - maybe it's drinking your coffee in the same spot each morning, or having a wind-down routine before bed.

Build in time for activities that help your nervous system regulate. This might be walking, yoga, reading, gardening, or any activity that helps you feel calm and present. These aren't luxuries - they're essential maintenance for your mental health, just like brushing your teeth is essential maintenance for your physical health.

Pay attention to work-life balance. If your work constantly keeps your nervous system activated - through unrealistic deadlines, toxic relationships, or values that don't match yours - it will be much harder to heal. While you might not be able to change everything about your work situation immediately, look for small ways to reduce stress and advocate for your needs.

Financial security plays a big role in feeling safe. Money isn't everything, but having enough to meet your basic needs helps your nervous system relax. If money is tight, focus on building small amounts of savings when you can, learning about resources available to you, and making choices that move you toward more financial stability over time.

Your physical health and mental health are connected. Taking care of your body - through movement, good food, enough sleep, and medical care when needed - supports your emotional healing. You don't need to be perfect with any of these things. Small, consistent choices add up over time.

Many people find that having some kind of spiritual practice or sense of meaning helps their healing journey. This doesn't have to be religious - it might be spending time in nature, volunteering for causes you care about, creative expression, or any practice that helps you feel connected to something bigger than your daily struggles.

If you're a woman, there are specific challenges and considerations for building a safe life. Women often face unique pressures and dangers that men don't have to think about as much.

In dating and romantic relationships, trust your instincts about safety. If someone pressures you sexually, doesn't respect your boundaries, or makes you feel like you have to be someone you're not, these are red flags. A healthy partner will support your healing journey, not make it harder.

In your career, you might face additional challenges around being taken seriously, workplace harassment, or balancing career growth with other responsibilities. Learn to advocate for yourself professionally while protecting your energy. This might mean speaking up about unfair treatment, asking for what you need, or sometimes

choosing opportunities that align better with your wellbeing over those that just look impressive.

If you become a mother, remember that taking care of
your own nervous system isn't selfish - it's one of the best
gifts you can give your children. Children learn more from
what they observe than what they're told. When they see
you treating yourself with kindness and maintaining
boundaries, they learn that they deserve the same treatment.

Advocate for yourself in healthcare settings. Many wom-
en's health concerns are dismissed or minimized. Trust
your own experience of your body and don't be afraid to
ask questions, seek second opinions, or find providers
who take your concerns seriously.

Work toward economic independence when possible.
Having your own financial resources gives you choices
and reduces dependence on others who might not have
your best interests at heart. This might happen slowly
over time, and that's okay. Every step toward independence is a step toward safety.

Healing isn't a straight line, and building a safe life is an
ongoing process. There will be times when stress increases, when old patterns resurface, or when life throws

you curveballs that challenge your nervous system. This doesn't mean you've failed or that your healing wasn't real. It means you're human.

Learn to recognize the early signs that your nervous system is getting activated. Maybe you start having trouble sleeping, or you notice yourself getting irritated more easily, or you start isolating from people you care about. When you catch these signs early, you can take action to support yourself before things get harder.

Have a plan for stressful periods. Know what helps you most when you're struggling - whether that's reaching out to specific people, doing certain activities, or using particular coping tools. Write this plan down when you're feeling good so you can refer to it when your brain is stressed and not thinking clearly.

Stay curious about your own patterns and growth. Keep learning about trauma, healing, and what helps you thrive. Your understanding will deepen over time, and you'll discover new things about yourself and what you need.

Celebrate your progress, even when it feels small. Healing happens in tiny moments - the time you spoke up for yourself, the day you chose rest instead of pushing through exhaustion, the moment you asked for help instead of suffering alone. These moments matter more than you might realize.

Humans are wired for connection, and part of building a safe life is finding your people - the communities where you can be yourself and contribute your unique gifts to the world.

Look for trauma-informed communities - groups of people who understand that everyone has struggles and that healing is possible. These might be support groups, online communities, spiritual congregations, hobby groups, or volunteer organizations. The key is finding places where you can be authentic without judgment.

Learn to balance independence and interdependence. Healing often requires becoming more independent - learning to trust yourself, meet your own needs, and not rely on others to regulate your emotions. But humans also need each other. Healthy interdependence means being able to give and receive support while maintaining your own sense of self.

Consider how your healing journey might help others. This doesn't mean you have to become a therapist or share your story publicly. It might mean being a good friend to someone else who's struggling, volunteering for causes you care about, or simply modeling healthy boundaries and self-care for the people around you.

Think about what kind of world you want to help create. Your healing work isn't just personal - it's also social. When you break cycles of trauma and create safety in your own life, you're contributing to a world where more people can thrive.

Building a safe life isn't a one-time project - it's an ongoing practice that grows and changes as you do. Schedule regular check-ins with yourself to see how you're doing and what might need adjustment.

Maybe once a month, ask yourself: How is my nervous system doing overall? Are there areas of my life that are causing more stress than they need to? What's working well that I want to keep doing? What small changes might help me feel even better?

Keep learning and growing. Read books, take classes, try new healing practices, or work with new therapists or coaches as your needs change. Stay curious about yourself and the world around you.

Remember that setbacks are part of the process, not signs of failure. If you find yourself slipping back into old patterns or struggling more than usual, treat yourself with the same kindness you'd show a good friend. Ask what you need in this moment and how you can support yourself through the difficulty.

Take some time to imagine what your life could look like as your nervous system continues to heal. What would you do if you felt truly safe in the world? What relationships would you pursue? What dreams would you chase? What kind of person would you become?

This isn't about creating pressure or expectations. It's about giving your nervous system a vision of safety and possibility to move toward. Your brain needs hope and direction to keep doing the hard work of healing.

Set goals that align with your healed self, not your traumatized self. Instead of goals based on proving yourself or avoiding rejection, set goals based on what would bring you joy, meaning, and authentic connection.

Think about the legacy you want to create through your healing work. This might be the relationships you build, the children you raise, the work you do, or simply the example you set for others that healing is possible.

As you continue to grow and learn, remember that you don't have to have everything figured out. Life is a journey of ongoing discovery. The goal isn't to reach some perfect destination where you never struggle again. The goal is to build a life where you can handle whatever comes your way with grace, wisdom, and self-compassion.

You deserve to live in a world that supports your wellbeing. You deserve relationships that nourish you, spaces that feel safe, work that has meaning, and a daily life that honors both your struggles and your strength. Building this kind of life takes time, patience, and lots of self-compassion, but it's absolutely possible.

Your nervous system has been protecting you for so long. Now you get to create a life where it can finally relax, knowing that you're truly safe. This is the greatest gift you can give yourself - and through your healing, you're also contributing to a world where others can feel safe too.

The journey continues, but you're no longer walking it alone. You have tools, wisdom, and the growing trust that you can handle whatever life brings your way. That's not just healing - that's transformation. And you've earned every bit of peace and joy that lies ahead.

Acknowledgments

Writing this book has been one of the most vulnerable and meaningful journeys I've ever taken, and it wouldn't have been possible without the incredible people who walked alongside me.

To the brave women who shared their stories with me—your courage to speak your truth, your questions that kept me digging deeper, and your honest moments of exhaustion and hope became the soul of these pages. You showed me that healing isn't about having it all figured out. It's about showing up, even when your nervous system is screaming that it's not safe to do so.

To my closest friends and chosen family—thank you for holding space when I couldn't find my words, for gently reminding me that rest isn't earned but needed, and for loving me through the messy, imperfect process of becoming. You've shown me what safety in relationships actually looks like, and that knowledge lives in every chapter of this book.

To the healers, teachers, and researchers whose work lit the path—thank you for dedicating your lives to understanding trauma and the nervous system. Your wisdom made it possible for me to translate complex concepts into words that could reach hearts that need healing.

And to you, dear reader—thank you for picking up this book, for trusting me with your precious time and maybe even your pain. Thank you for being willing to look at your nervous system with curiosity instead of judgment, and for believing that feeling safe in your own body is possible. If these words helped you understand yourself better, feel less alone, or take even one small step toward healing, then every vulnerable moment of writing was worth it.

This book exists because there are people like you in the world—people who are tired of just surviving, ready to understand why their brain won't let them feel safe, and brave enough to do the work of healing. Your willingness to grow and heal creates ripples that touch everyone around you.

With deep gratitude and hope for your healing journey,

Rowan Blake

www.ingramcontent.com/pod-product-compliance
Ingram Content Group UK Ltd.
Pitfield, Milton Keynes, MK11 3LW, UK
UKHW021306281025
8640UKWH00030B/413